Just Right

Discover the Best Business Idea for YOU

By Rachael L. Thompson

© Copyright 2016 by Mind Body & Spirit Entrepreneur - All rights reserved.

Disclaimer
This document is geared towards providing exact and reliable information in regards to the topic and issue covered. The publication is sold with the idea that the publisher is not required to render accounting, officially permitted, or otherwise, qualified services. If advice is necessary, legal or professional, a practiced individual in the profession should be ordered.

- From a Declaration of Principles which was accepted and approved equally by a Committee of the American Bar Association and a Committee of Publishers and Associations.

This book is intended for entertainment purposes only. The views expressed here are those of the author alone and should not be taken as expert instruction or command. The reader is responsible for his or her own actions.

In no way is it legal to reproduce, duplicate, or transmit any part of this document in either electronic means or in printed format. Recording of this publication is strictly prohibited and any storage of this document is not allowed unless with written permission from the publisher. All rights reserved.

The information provided herein is stated to be truthful and consistent, in that any liability, in terms of inattention or otherwise, by any usage or abuse of any policies, processes, or directions contained within is the solitary and utter responsibility of the recipient reader. Under no circumstances will any legal responsibility or blame be held against the publisher for any reparation, damages, or monetary loss due to the information herein, either directly or indirectly.

Respective authors own all copyrights not held by the publisher.

The information herein is offered for informational purposes solely, and is universal as so. The presentation of the information is without contract or any type of guarantee assurance.

The trademarks that are used are without any consent, and the publication of the trademark is without permission or backing by the trademark owner. All trademarks and brands within this book are for clarifying purposes only and are the owned by the owners themselves, not affiliated with this document.

Introduction

If you have dreamed about starting a business but have little idea where to start, this is the book for you. Are you nervous about high startup failure rates, lack of business knowledge or the potential of losing a lot of money? Or do you want to become an entrepreneur but have no business ideas? This book will address all of these areas and set you up with a plan for success. Too often new entrepreneurs blindly start businesses without fully understanding what they are getting into. After reading this, you will have a clear picture of the main components (money, time, growth potential, etc.) of different types of businesses so that you are able to prevent unnecessary stress and set yourself and your future business up for success.

In this book you will find 10 different types of businesses you can open. Each chapter is simply structured, first explaining what the business is, then listing examples of specific types of businesses, followed by a list of the pros and cons of running that kind of business. If you are interested or curious about starting a business, this book will help you figure out what option is right for you and some possible ways to start and manage your perfect business.

People are often looking for the "best" business idea, and frankly, there is no such thing. What this book will do, is help clarify the best business idea(s) for you. You will likely be familiar with some of the businesses listed while others may be completely new concepts. Use this as a starting point. You can then further research ideas that sound appealing to you. If you are worried about finances, stress, lack of time or lack of business knowledge, this book will guide you through which business will be the least worrisome for you to explore. Feel free to only read about the businesses that sound the most interesting to you, but I recommend reading through all descriptions as you may find something you never thought of before.

Table of Contents

Introduction to Types of Income Streams: Active vs. Passive..................1

Chapter 1: Bricks and Mortar......................4

Chapter 2: Online and Home Based...............9

Chapter 3: Buy Existing Business or Franchise......................................15

Chapter 4: Creative Business......................17

Chapter 5: Affiliate Marketing/Internet Marketing..22

Chapter 6: Selling Products.........................26

Chapter 7: Service Based.............................29

Chapter 8: Information Based.....................33

Chapter 9: Better way to do things.................37

Chapter 10: Non-Profit..................................41

Chapter 11: Recap...44

Conclusion..47

About the Author..51

Introduction to Types of Income Streams: Active vs. Passive

Before we can get into the list of businesses, two main business concepts need to be discussed. These concepts will be referred to as "Active" and "Passive" business models and will be used when describing the types of businesses throughout the book.

Active/Traditional Income: The Direct Exchange of Time for Money

When you think of an entrepreneur or a business owner, what are some businesses that come to mind? Could it be somebody who runs a big company, somebody who is in real estate, somebody who owns a restaurant, a salon, a boutique, a store, a gas station? These are more traditional or active ways to run in a business. *This means that there is direct exchange of time for money.* If you own a salon, somebody has to be there styling and cutting hair for your business to make money. If you run a clothing boutique, somebody has to be there selling clothes while customers are buying them; the owner is also likely there, managing employees or possibly selling directly to customers. The business does not make any money unless there are actual people running the business.

Passive Income: The Non-Direct Method of Earning Profits

The second way that you can run your business is labeled "Passive", in which you earn income without the direct exchange of your time. This does not mean you do nothing and just start making money; it describes a business model in which a business provides a product or a service that can be purchased without the owner or an employee's immediate involvement. That product or service continues to make you money even when you are not technically doing anything. It might sound confusing if you have not heard the term before, so let's look at a couple of examples:

Example 1: Blog Writers/Content Creators: Those who earn money from writing blogs through advertising or affiliate marketing (if you are unfamiliar with those terms we will be going over them in this book). Blog writers can spend a lot of time writing a blog. They might spend two weeks writing a really great blog, but after it's published online, they don't have to do anything. They are getting money because they set up structures to get paid through the material they wrote.

Example 2: Authors: Those who write books, fiction or non-fiction, and publish with a publisher or self-publish online. Authors can spend years writing a book, requiring a lot of time and energy. After it is written they have to then spend additional time and energy promoting that book. But after that period of time, they make money without directly selling to customers. They do not have to be at bookstores, handing the book to customers to make the money.

Example 3: Application (App) Developers: Those who create a computer or mobile program, either through developing it themselves or hiring an outside contractor to develop it. Think of Apps you have paid for on your phone or tablet. The person who developed that App was not there directly selling it to you, yet still made money when you purchased it.

In the list below of 10 different businesses there will be plenty of examples of ways to earn both passive and active income.

Chapter 1: Bricks and Mortar

What is it?

Bricks and mortar is a term used to refer to a physical location. Do you want an actual location for your business? Do you need an actual location for the type of business you want to open?

Examples:

Restaurant/Bar

Store/Boutique

Service location: (Provides a service) Example: Salon, Dog Groomer, Daycare

Pros

1. Can be only one in your area: You can monopolize an area if you open a business that has no competition. For example, in some small towns people have to travel to another community to pick up groceries. If one was to open a small grocery store in this area there would be zero competition for miles.

2. Meet the need of a demand that is not being met: Similar to being the only business in your area, you can also meet a need that is not being met by competitors. Perhaps you have noticed an increase in health awareness among citizens of your community. They opened a new gym that has been wildly successful, but there are still only the same unhealthy restaurant options. If you opened a place that served

healthy food options you can meet a growing need that has not yet been met in your market.

3. Meet the demand in a different way than is currently being met: Perhaps there are similar businesses already open in your area. This can be good because it shows that there is a need for the business you want to open. If you can differentiate yourself and meet demands that the other businesses are not meeting, then it can become very profitable. For example, there is only 1 coffee shop in your area and they have very limited options. If you open a coffee shop that provides a variety of new specialty drinks, it will draw customers looking for this.

4. Ability to work with your hands, be face-to-face with people and engaged in the community: If working within your community is important to you then bricks and mortar is the way to go. You get daily face-to-face interaction and the ability to hear customer feedback.

5. Easier to drive traffic than online stores: With proper signage and a good location, you can cut a lot of money and time out of marketing efforts. Think about a business that you went into just because it seemed enticing. What drew you to this place? If you can replicate similar signage and characteristics, you likely will draw in customers as well. It is much easier to drive traffic to a bricks and mortar location than to online businesses. Happy customers also equal free advertising as they tell their friends and family about your location.

Cons

1. High overhead and start-up costs: Bricks and mortar businesses are often the most expensive to both start and run. There are many costs including rent, utilities, inventory, and insurance coverage that add up quickly. There is pressure to be able to make a certain amount of money each month in order to simply keep your business open.

2. Might have to get loans, investors, borrow from friends and family: Because of the high start-up costs, many business owners have to borrow money. The process of borrowing money can be highly stressful and can also push back your open date.

3. Can cause extra pressure to make profits immediately and run your business in a particular way: Depending on who you borrow money from, there may be input from investors on how your business will be run. There is also an added pressure to run your business in a way that will generate profits immediately so you are able to pay back the money.

4. Finding the perfect location: Finding a location for your business that is both in your price range and a desired location can be extremely difficult. Some have to postpone their business ideas for months or even years until they are able to find this location. Additionally, there may not be a need for the business you want to run in the area you live. Are you willing to move to start your business in an area where

the demand is higher? If you open a business that does not meet a need in your area, it will not be successful. This is why proper market research needs to be done prior.

5. Large time commitment: Before opening a business, you will need to decide what your role will be. Will you be a manager, an employee, a marketing specialist, an operations director, or all of the above? If you plan to start a smaller business with only a few employees, you will be required to spend a lot of time at your business. If someone calls out sick, you will cover the shift, and if someone quits, you will cover their shifts until you find a replacement. Are you ready to always be on call? It is a good idea to talk to other owners who run similar businesses to get an idea of the time commitment that is required.

6. Cost of renovations and upkeep: When budgeting for both start-up and overhead costs, you must include renovations and repairs. It is also something to think about when looking for a location. Renovations can not only be expensive, but also very time consuming. It can take months to get a business to the place it should be, and often you have to pay for rent before you are able to open your doors. (Every leasing agreement is different and this should be considered and negotiated). Along with the initial renovations, there must be a budget to pay for any repairs that are needed. This is also something to think about before leasing or

purchasing a location. Hope for the best, but prepare for the worse.

7. Cost of employees: Unless you plan to be the sole worker in your businesses, you will need to pay employees. There are considerations when dealing with payroll, workers comp, insurance, etc. Also you will need to decide if you will hire managers to help run the business. Will they be hourly or salary? The more you expect of your employees, the more you will have to pay them. The worst feeling business owners experience is not having enough money to pay their employees. Budgeting properly during your financial planning will help prevent this unfortunate situation.

Chapter 2: Online and Home Based

What is it?

This is a business that is based solely online or can be added as a component of a bricks and mortar location.

Two Platforms:

There are essentially two ways to run an online business. The first is to have your own website. This may seem daunting if you are not tech savvy, but there are plenty of platforms available that are user friendly as well as professionals who build websites.

The second option is to use a platform (eBay/Amazon) that customers use to make purchases. There are pros and cons to each of these. The biggest hurdle with having your own website is driving traffic to it. This is why many people start out using a third party platform that already has high volume and consistent traffic. The downsides of using platforms are you must follow their rules, have less freedom, as well as have to share your profits with that platform.

Examples:

Online (Ecommerce) Stores: Any store that customers shop and purchase products online

Creative and Information Products: A blog, videos, music, art work, courses

Services: Life coach, digital marketing, nutrition counseling, consulting. These are services that you likely will provide via phone or internet (ex. Skype) and you can work from anywhere.

Dropshipping: Selling products that are manufactured and stored in another location and are shipped to your customers directly when they purchase from your website. This means that you, the store owner, never touch the products. There are a lot of companies that will provide these services at a cost.

Using platforms like eBay, Amazon, Etsy to sell: There are multiple options for selling on these platforms, and each one has its own rules and regulations. In general you can sell your own products, use dropshipping, use inventory from manufacturers, or write and self-publish books (on Amazon). Each website has more information on what is allowed on that site.

Pros

1. Can be much cheaper: The start-up costs are typically far less expensive than opening a bricks and mortar location. With average computer knowledge and a little amount of money, anyone can build a website. If you have an idea for a bricks and mortar location but are worried about finances, this could be a wise alternative. Since you do not have to worry about keeping a location open, you often do not have to have employees or as many employees as are needed for bricks and mortar.

2. Can reach a larger audience, a more diverse audience, and meet needs of people all over the world. (Might not be a need in your

neighborhood, but is in other parts of the world): If you have an idea but there is not a need in your area, the internet can be the perfect place to find customers. For example, if you have an idea for the perfect yoga mat, but there are no yoga studios in your area, there is still a large number of people around the world who could be very interested in your product idea.

3. Can start and run a business from anywhere and freedom in schedule: You have a lot more freedom in online businesses. You do not have to work a set schedule, work from a certain location, or deal with daily rush hour traffic. Depending on the type of business you run, you can work from anywhere in the world as long as there is an internet connection.

4. There are plenty of tools making it easy for those who are not tech savvy to open and run various types of online businesses: There are plenty of website platforms that allow you to start your website for free and then pay a monthly or yearly amount. There is free marketing via social media and many have built entire businesses using only these platforms. Email marketing is another valuable, low-cost option. Similar to website platforms, there are email marketing companies that allow you to use their services for free until you have a certain amount of email subscribers. There is also tons of free information available online to teach you how to run and market your online business. Just

look at popular blogs and YouTube channels related to your niche.

5. Can be passive or active: Whether your business is passive or active is determined by both the type of online business you run and the systems you put in place. There are automatic programs that you can put in place to make your business more passive. Online business owners often hire Virtual Assistants to handle much of the day-to-day tasks, making the business more passive. If you want to save money or take a more active role in your business, then it will require more of your time. Inventory is another factor that determines if your business will be passive or active. If you use a dropshipping company, this is passive, but if you store, package and ship your own inventory, this requires an active approach.

6. Great place to start to test an idea before spending too much money: Online businesses are typically the best way start small because of the low overhead that is required. You can start it part-time while keeping your current job, eliminating much of the financial anxiety that new entrepreneurs face. If you are selling products, you can keep a low inventory until you have sales. It also provides an opportunity to make mistakes and learn without wasting a lot of money doing so.

Cons

1. Hard to drive traffic: It is much harder to drive traffic, and conversion rates are considerably

lower in online businesses than in bricks and mortar businesses. Without knowing how to drive traffic to a website through SEO (search engine optimization) and various other advertising and marketing strategies, it is probable that nobody will know your business even exists.

2. You have to spend a lot of time and money focusing on producing free content, such as blogging, or marketing on various online platforms to bring in customers: People are often skeptical of online businesses at first, especially if they do not know anyone else who has purchased from that business before. There are various ways to build this trust, but all of these ways involve your time. At first, expect to spend a lot of time on your business without financial compensation in return.

3. There will be a lot of competition that you may not have when opening a bricks and mortar location, as you are competing with everyone in you niche online: You are competing with everyone else online, including large companies that can spend millions on driving traffic and marketing. You need to not only know ways to drive traffic, but figure out a way to differentiate yourself from all of the competition.

4. Working from home can become isolating and difficult to stay on track: If you are the type who needs a manager or set schedule to be productive, starting an online business will

pose some challenges. There are also a lot of tasks that need to be accomplished each day and it can be difficult to prioritize them. Also, for those that need frequent contact with others, working from home can get very lonely.

Chapter 3: Buy Existing Business or Franchise

What is it?

To buy an Existing Business is to purchase a business that is already established. This can be bricks and mortar or online.

Example: Buy the local bakery from Bob, who is 80 and wants to retire.

To buy a Franchise is to buy into an existing name, and as the investor or franchisee, and are thus able to run this business.

Federal Trade Commission states: "A franchise enables you, the investor or franchisee, to operate a business. You pay a franchise fee and you get a format or system developed by the company (franchisor), the right to use the franchisor's name for a specific number of years and assistance. For example, the franchisor may provide you with help in finding a location for your outlet; initial training and an operating manual; and advice on management, marketing or personnel. The franchisor may provide support through periodic newsletters, a toll-free telephone number, a website or scheduled workshops or seminars." (www.ftc.gov)

Example: Jimmy John's

If you are interested in which franchise would be right for you (based on investment), take a look at Forbes 2016 List of Best Franchises.

Pros

Buy a Business: Established name, initial marketing set-up, existing customer base, can review business records before buying to know revenue, sometimes can be easier to obtain funding (depending on track record).

Franchise: Become part of a well-known image and name, highly structured, get training and guidance, can turn to other franchisees for help if needed.

Cons

Buy a Business: There can be misrepresentations about profits, acquired debts and loans, can have a bad reputation, might not be able to make changes you would like without backlash from loyal customers, employees can be used to a particular management and resistant to change, no guarantee it will be a success.

Franchise: Not a lot of freedom, need a lot of capital, ongoing royalties and fees, some contracts limit ability to exit a business, franchisor's problems will affect your business.

TAKE HOME POINT: Get professional help (lawyer) when entering either one of these businesses.

Chapter 4: Creative Business

What is it?

A business in which you create something in exchange for money.

You will need to consider one major factor when you are developing your business plan: Do you create something that can be replicated (digital prints, books, music downloads, blogs), or do you physically need to create the products (jewelry, crafts, etc.)? This will determine if it is passive or active. If you create a book, you only have to write that book once and can sell as many copies as people want to buy. If you make custom jewelry, you can physically only create one piece at a time. One is not better than the other, but you must think about this when deciding pricing as well as planning what your role in the company will look like.

Examples:

Sell Crafts on Etsy or Own Website: Jewelry, Wedding Products, Home Décor, Clothing, Toys and Games

Write and Self-Publish Novels: Kindle Direct Publishing (Amazon), Nook, iTunes, Smashwords, Createspace

Blogging: Travel, Food, Fashion, Animals

Art: Sell online or in-person at galleries, events, festivals, etc.

Music: Can sell digitally on own website or third party platforms, can post on YouTube (look up Patreon to see how to get financial support from fans for your work)

Pros

1. Can turn your passion into income and get to do what you love: Creative people feel alive when they are in the process of crafting their masterpieces. In today's world, there are plenty of outlets to showcase all forms of creation. If you can figure out a way to make your creative works profitable, you are able to do what most cannot, make a living doing something that you love every day.

2. Creative freedom: When you own a business, you are able to call the shots. It can be creatively stifling to work in a job in which others dictate what you can and cannot create. If you own a business, you have creative control. Since most of this type of work is passive, you can also set your own schedule and work from anywhere.

3. Can develop very loyal customer base: There is a theory stating all you need to make a living is 1000 true fans. If you have a small number of people who buy all of your creations and recommend your work to their friends, you can be set. There are a wide variety of tastes and interest, all you have to do is find that group of people with whom your work resonates.

4. Can start small and scale: You are able to start small and test several ideas to see which one sticks. For example, you can self-publish 10

different types of short novels on Amazon, iTunes, Nook, etc. to see which one gets the most sales and then create a series based on your most popular book. Or you can start selling on Etsy and then develop your own website and eventually open a bricks and mortar boutique with your jewelry. You can start selling art at farmers markets or festivals and handout cards with your website, email or social media site to stay in contact with potential customers and build a following. The possibilities are endless.

Cons

1. Will need to have customers who want to pay for your product: Have you ever heard the expression "starving artist"? This comes from the reality in which many creatives produce pieces that they love, but are not necessarily loved by the general public (at that time). If you want to create and make money from your creative work you will need to make sure you are crafting something that people are willing to pay money for. If not, it is a hobby, not a business.

2. People may not see your vision: You may, and likely will, have to deal with haters. It can be devastating to hear nasty comments made about something you poured your heart and soul into. There is a balance between being able to take constructive criticism to help grow and also be able to ignore people who are just being negative. It is better to be loved by some than

to be liked by all, because it is those who love what you do who will buy from you. Those who think you're okay, will say "That's nice" but will never open their wallets. So put yourself out there and let the controversy begin.

3. Will need to market and get name out there: Often the number one problem that creative business owners make is lack of marketing. You have to understand marketing concepts and strategies, know who your target market is, and devise a plan of how you are going to reach out to potential customers. This may involve doing some things that are out of your comfort zone and evoke fear and anxiety. Do not let this prevent you from trying. There is a lot of free information available to help and if you have the funds you can also hire someone to help you with this.

4. Can be a large time investment: As mentioned previously, it can take a while to establish trust with potential customers. A popular theory states that it take 7 "touches" with your business before the average person will purchase. This could be that they read a blog article, see you on social media, join your email list and receive several emails, and watch a YouTube video all before they feel comfortable enough to invest their money in what you are offering. Or possibly they see your work at four different art shows before they take your card and follow you on Facebook and after following you for three months decide to purchase a piece of art. This means that you have to invest

a lot of time reaching out to establish this trust. If you truly are doing something you love, this will not seem as overwhelming as it first sounds. If you are proud of your work then share it on all platforms. Depending on your personality this may or may not be comfortable, but it is a must to turn your creations into products people will pay for.

5. The hassle of selling products: If you are creating physical products, you will need a place to store supplies, make products, deal with shipping (if it is online) and have enough overhead capital to pay for product supplies until you make a profit. Customers today are used to instant gratification, so you also must consider how long it will take to create products. Always be upfront and do not make promises you cannot keep. People would rather know it will take 4 weeks to get a product than you stating it will take 1 week and it taking a month.

Chapter 5: Affiliate Marketing/Internet Marketing

What is it?

A business in which you earn income by promoting products or services offered by others. You do not need to make a product or service. This is often how content creators earn money.

Examples of Affiliate Marketing: Amazon Affiliates (Promote Amazon products and get commission), Individual Affiliate Programs (On business websites)

If you have a blog, this can be an excellent way to capitalize. Search for websites that offer products and services in your niche. Many websites have an "Affiliate Program" link that is often located at the bottom of the Home Page. Even if they do not have this, you can contact the company and ask. Once you become an affiliate, you will receive an affiliate link. Write about the products or services in your content and provide the affiliate links. Each time a reader clicks on a link and buys a product or service, you get a percentage of the profits. For example, if you have a blog that is about dogs, you can suggest dog services and products and get paid every time a reader purchases one of these.

Examples of Internet Marketing: Banner Ads, Pay Per Click Advertisements, Targeted Emails

It is your decision where you want to place these ads on your website or blog. Every time someone clicks on an ad that is on your website you will get a certain amount of money for this. This approach can come off as more sales-like than the Affiliate Marketing.

Pros

1. You do not need to worry about developing a product or service: You never have to worry about inventory, production, fulfilling orders, customer complaints, and all the other potentially frustrating parts about owning a business.

2. Inexpensive: This is one of the cheapest, if not the cheapest, way to start and run a business. Costs vary depending on how you set up your marketing strategies, but most likely all you need is a website, email marketing service, and social media platforms. All of these can be free or cost as little as 5-10 dollars a month.

3. Is a great way to support your creative business: By adding affiliate links to your blogs or website you are able to make money from what you create. If you always wanted to start a blog but did not know how you would make money from it, this is the way to go! You can have advertisements on your website, write about products or services and provide affiliate links, and/or have a "Resource" page on your website with your recommended products and services related to your niche (the topic you write about) and provide affiliate links to all of these resources. Before starting a blog, it is a great idea to line up some affiliate links so that you are able to start making money immediately.

4. Can work from anywhere/Freedom in schedule: Since you are not providing customers with products or services you have complete freedom in your schedule and location.

5. Large income potential (if done right): The top affiliate and internet marketers have made millions. This attracts a lot of people to this field. However, the results are not typical and many fail to make an income. If you have marketing experience and/or if you are extremely passionate about the information that you provide you can become successful. If you do not want to put a lot of effort into your business, this may not be the field for you.

Cons

1. Need to have customers to refer to affiliate offers: If you have a blog, you need blog readers in order to make money. If you have a website, you must have large amounts of daily traffic to make money. If you want to make money from advertisements, businesses must be willing to pay to put their advertisements on your website.

2. Knowledge of SEO (Search Engine Optimization - How you rank in search engines): If you have never heard of this term and you are interested in this type of business, take some time to familiarize yourself with the strategies involved in improving SEO. This essentially means that if someone types in keywords pertaining to your niche in a search

engine, your website or blog article will show up on Google, Yahoo, Bing, etc. It is not easy to rank, especially with a new website. Learning these techniques, paying for services, and taking time to improve SEO can deter some from embarking on this type of business.

3. No control over products or services: Customers may blame you if they had an unpleasant experience with something that you referred. If you are trying to build a brand that people trust, it is wise to only recommend products or services you know your customers will like. You can either try them yourself or do thorough research before recommending.

4. Competition and commissions vary drastically (can be very low): Since this is fairly easy to run and has a large income potential, there are a lot of people trying this to make a quick buck. You will need to set yourself apart from these competitors. Not every product or niche will be lucrative, and you may only receive a few cents every time a customer purchases a particular item you recommended. Research and planning will help you make the most out of this type of business.

Chapter 6: Selling Products

What is it?

The selling of physical products online, in a store, or at markets or events. There are a lot of different ways to run a product-based business. Begin to ask yourself the following questions to become clearer on what your business may look like:

Will you create the products? Will you have the products manufactured? Will you purchase the products from a manufacturer or wholesaler? Will you be selling to businesses (B2B) or customers (B2C)? (If you manufacture or import products from overseas you can either sell to distributors or wholesalers who sell products to retailers or you can sell directly to customers.) Where will you store your products? Will your manufacturer be in your country or outside of your country? Will you sell in a store, an online store and/or a platform, like Amazon, Etsy or eBay? (You can have multiple sales channels to increase profit potential.) Doing just a little online research in this area can help further your understanding of all the options available to you.

Selling products can be passive or active. Dropshipping is fairly passive, but creating and selling products by hand is very active.

Pros

Note: Keep in mind that all of these types of business models will have entirely different pricing and marketing strategies as well as costs associated with them. Making a product from scratch and selling it directly to customers online will look very different than importing products from overseas and selling them to businesses. For this reason, the pros and cons vary.

1. Can turn ideas into profit: Too many people have great ideas but do not think it is feasible to turn these ideas into actual products and sell them. There are plenty of manufacturers inside and outside the US who can turn your ideas into actual products.

2. Creative: This can be the perfect business for someone who is creative and enjoys designing.

3. Can be lucrative: You can make a lot of money selling products. This varies drastically with every business, and you will need to think of all overhead costs when making a business plan.

4. Lots and lots of options, bricks and mortar, online, both. Passive or Active: The possibilities are endless and you can find something that matches both your interests and your budget.

5. Dropshipping products can be very inexpensive (A manufacturer or wholesaler directly ships products to customers): As mentioned previously, dropshipping can be an excellent way to make money and build a brand with very little start-up costs.

Cons

1. Can be high overhead to produce initial products: You may have to purchase a large

inventory and/or pay a lot for product manufacturing before you make any profits.

2. Patents and legal fees can be expensive and time consuming: If you are creating a product, you have to look into getting the proper patent. You can research this on your own, but talking to a professional patent lawyer is highly suggested.

3. Need a place to manufacture and store products: This can be time consuming as well as expensive.

4. Need to track inventory: It can be hard to know how much to purchase or manufacture and how much to keep in stock. It is often a learning curve that can be frustrating for both business owners and customers.

5. If creating products, will need testing and modifications: You will need to get product samples before you can mass produce your product. This can also be expensive and time consuming, especially if your manufacturer is outside of your country.

Chapter 7: Service Based

What is it?

Provide service in exchange for payment. It can be B2B or B2C, meaning that you can offer your services to other businesses or directly to customers. When considering a service-based business, consider the following:

Is there a need for this, and are people willing to pay? This will often be determined by your location. For example, opening a surf school in Ohio likely will not be as lucrative of a business as opening one in Florida.

Is it evergreen or temporary? Think of businesses you saw as a kid that slowly went extinct as times changed. As our environment and situation changes, so do our needs. If you can find a service that people will always need or a service that can be flexible and change with the times, you can be set for lifelong success.

Is it a one-time need or frequent? If you provide a service that people will only need once (example: a new mommy class) you will constantly need to acquire new customers, but if you provide a service that people will need again (a mechanic) then you can rely on loyal customers to keep your business running.

One thing to keep in mind is that service based businesses are mainly active because your time is needed. Can be passive if you manage employees who provide the service, but likely you will still need to be present to provide the management.

Examples:

Car Services (repair, washing)

Home Owners Services (cleaning, lawn care)

Child Care (daycare, nanny)

Pet Care (sitting, grooming)

Grooming (hair dresser, make-up artist, spa)

Wellness (personal trainer, nutritionist, health coach)

Professional (accountant, lawyer)

Freelance (writer, graphic designer)

Pros

1. Can turn your skills or trade into a profitable business: There are a lot of business success stories of people who began by providing their services to friends and family for free and turned it into a business. An example is a violinist who started playing at events as a favor and turned it into a lucrative business through word of mouth and local advertising.

2. Can start small and scale. (Start part-time if needed): You can always start with friends and family, get their testimonials, and use this to slowly build a business. You can do work during your free time, while keeping your current job. Party/Event planners often start this way.

3. Often can make own schedule (but has to still meet needs of client): You will likely not have to work a 9-5 schedule and can let your clients know what hours you are available. This will

vary depending on your field. For example, a wedding planner will be required to work mostly weekends, a personal trainer will likely work around the client's work schedule (early mornings and evenings), and a tutor will have to work when children get out of school.

4. Can train others to work for you: Once you develop a standard practice for your services, you can hire others to perform the work and take a portion of their earnings. For example, a dog walker starts by walking dogs for money until she gets too many clients and then hires fellow walkers to work under her.

5. If it is a service that people use often, can rely on repeat customers for a lot of business to cut down on marketing: This can make running a business much easier after the initial client acquisition. All you need to do to keep clients is to provide quality services that meet their needs at a cost they are willing to pay. Also, these loyal customers can recommend your services and provide free advertising to build your business.

Cons

1. Mostly active, exchange your time for money: Depending on your field, it may be hard to take vacations during certain times, to work from anywhere, and to work limited hours. People will not pay for your service if you are unavailable to work at a time that they need your service. It is something to keep in mind when you are planning.

2. Carefully pick business model to make sure that you are able to have repeat customers: Example: If your business provides services for first time mothers, you will only get those customers once! Can you add other services to meet ongoing needs of your customers?

3. May have to deal with invoices. (You provide the service and bill customers): This means that you may not receive payment for weeks or even months after initial service. This can cause problems when paying employees and other overhead costs.

Chapter 8: Information Based

What is it?

Do you have extensive knowledge on a topic? You can capitalize on this by selling information products to customers.

Consider the following: What do you know about and who is your audience? What need is this information meeting? Why do people want to know this?

If you have definitive answers for all of the above questions, you likely have a great idea for an information-based business.

Examples:

Writing books: Can easily self-publish books on any topic.

Blogs: Use advertising/affiliate marketing to generate income or use blogs to drive traffic and sell books, courses, etc. to blog readers.

Producing YouTube videos: Can make money by funneling YouTube followers to other products, advertisements, and Pateron (a website that allows followers and fans to donate money to you).

Courses: Can sell on own website or third party sites like Udemy. Can also hold classes in own community.

Templates: If you can create a template that saves customers time and stress, they will pay!

Resource guides: Can sell on own website or make into a book and self-publish.

Pros

1. Turn your passion and knowledge into income: There are plenty of ways to share your knowledge with the world. Think of things that have helped you in your own life, and share that with others. Do not think you need a specialized degree or years of experience to start an information based business. Plenty of entrepreneurs have simply shared their journey with the world and made a living by teaching others to replicate what they did. For example, two moms were able to make a fulltime living off of green smoothie challenges just by sharing recipes and techniques that worked for them.

2. Several ways to generate income (Affiliate marketing, directly selling services and products, or both): There are multiple ways to generate income based on information. You could write a book, create an audible book and a course to sell all on one topic. You can also create a blog or email newsletter with affiliate links to generate income. Online courses have increased in popularity drastically over the past several years. There are platforms, such as Udemy, that you can become an instructor on or you can create a course on your own website.

3. Low costs: If you have a computer you can begin to share your knowledge for free. Even if you decide to build a website to sell your information based products the monthly overhead will be reasonably low. You do not even need a website when you use other

platforms such as Amazon. You can write a book and sell it on Amazon without spending a dime.

4. Often passive income: Once you create your information-based product you can sell copies of it while you sleep. The initial time spent to make a product can be substantial and you will need to spend time marketing it, but after that it will not be something that requires your constant attention.

5. Can often work from anywhere and have freedom over schedule: You can plan when you create and market your products and as long as you have a computer you will likely be able to work from anywhere.

Cons

1. Can be high competition (depending on niche): It seems as though everyone is an expert these days. With this field having the potential of a large, passive income it has attracted a lot of interest. You will need to figure out how you will differentiate yourself from others as well as devise an effective marketing plan.

2. Need to establish yourself as an authority and gain trust of customers: You will likely have to provide your products for free or at a low cost until you are able to establish trust. For example, if you create a course you can offer it for free to people in exchange for testimonials and feedback. Be prepared for people to look into and question your background so be

honest with the extent of training and experience you have in your field.

3. Often need to put out a lot of free content to build trust before people will buy from you: Just like many online businesses, you will need to produce free content (blogs, ebooks, videos) so that people will begin to trust you and be willing to pay for your products.

4. Need to be able to teach in a way that resonates with customers: Just because you know something does not mean that you will be able to effectively teach others. Often those who know a lot about a subject have trouble explaining the topic to others at a beginner level. Listen to feedback from customers to alter the way you explain things, if needed. Observe how others in your field teach or write about the information. You can even take courses yourself on how to teach others in an effective manner.

Chapter 9: Better way to do things

What is it?

This can be a service, a program, software or an app, or a product and is anything that makes your customer's life better, easier or saves time.

Do you have a great technique for _____?

Examples:

Cooking Services

Organizational Services

Phone Apps

Workout Plans

Computer Software

Pros

1. People will pay for things that make their lives easier: Figure out your potential customers' "pain points". This means areas that they struggle in or things that they hate doing. If you can offer solutions to these pains they will pay you money for it. An example could be parenting techniques for raising children with ADHD. Many parents are frustrated and feel lost. If you write a book or provide services to help them implement helpful techniques, many will take advantage of your services.

2. Can be passive or active: You can make this an information-based business or a service-based

business, or both. You can have a book and a blog but also offer coaching or consultation services. Apps and software programs can be downloaded months and years after you first develop them. You will have to continue to update and provide customer service, but these are primarily passive and potentially lucrative businesses.

3. Can turn things you do in your own life into money-making programs: Have your friends ever asked you how you do something? For example, how you always stay so organized, or how you manage to always eat healthy with such a busy lifestyle. These are opportunities to examine what you do differently or "better" than others and think of how you can teach others to do the same.

4. Inexpensive to start (depending on business): You could start a business like this with a simple email address or phone number that people can use to contact you. If you want to market your services online or in your community there can be costs associated with that, but you have the option to start small and invest money as the business begins to make a profit.

Cons

1. Needs to be a market: Your business needs to meet the needs of enough people to make a profit. Ask yourself, is this something that many people will pay for? Then ask others if they would pay for a service like the one you

are offering. Get as much information as you can about what people are struggling with so that you can effectively structure and market your services. For example, if you want to teach people a better way to handle stress at work there are plenty of different ways that you can do this. Find out what about work causes so much stress and make a program to address this in particular.

2. Can only have one time customers: If you solve your customers' problems they won't need to come back. You will have to consider this when devising a marketing strategy. You can always expand your business to create new products or services for returning customers or develop a plan for consistent new customer acquisitions (such as a referral program).

3. Can be time-consuming: If you provide services or classes then you will need to exchange your time for money. You may have to provide free consults in order to get sales or spend a great deal of time networking and meeting potential customers. At first, you may have to spend a lot of time without making a lot of money to acquire customers and establish a reputation.

4. Are you the only one who knows how to do this? Can you train others?: If you are the only one who knows these skills then you will be the sole member in your business. If you provide direct services then your business will be limited in its capacity to grow. Having a plan to

grow and teach others what you know will be beneficial to the growth of your company.

5. May not be able to scale or expand: There are many reasons why you would not be able to scale or expand, such as being a one-man-show, only offering one service, not being designed for repeat customers, or having a limited demographic. For example, if only you teach a new parent class in a community where the average age is 50 years old you may not be able to scale. You will have to target the few new parents but they will be one-time customers. Also, if only you are able to teach this, it will likely require a lot of your time to do consults, travel and teach without a lot of time left to market or plan for expansion.

Chapter 10: Non-Profit

What is it?

A corporation that conducts business for the good of the general public without shareholders and without a profit motive

Are created according to state law and must go through the same steps as many for-profit organizations (fees, applying for articles of organization, etc.)

Examples:

Check out Charity Navigator to get ideas of what is already out there. This website lists charities, rates them and gives information about their revenue and expenses.

Animals: Protect and provide services for domestic and wild animals

Arts and Culture: Promote and preserve artistic and cultural excellence

Community: Promote economic growth and stability

Environment: Preserve and protect the environment

Education: Make learning possible for students of all ages

Health and Human Service: Provide services to people in need

Human Rights: Designed to promote and protect reform

International: Work throughout the world to promote peace and service

Religion: Support religions and religious activity

Research: Focus on advancement of knowledge in a variety of fields

Pros

1. May qualify for government or foundational grants: This is likely how you will get some of your funding.
2. Protected from liability for directors and business
3. You can pay salaries to employees: You can pay yourself (if you are an employee) and other employees a salary as well as have volunteers.
4. People will volunteer: The more volunteers you have, the more of the funding can go into the non-profit because they provide service without payment.
5. Can make a huge difference in the world!

Cons

1. It can be stressful obtaining funding (grant applications, getting donations, etc.): It can be very time consuming and stressful to look and apply for grants. Also, a lot of time will be spent planning different ways to get donations from the community. You have to sell your mission as if it were a product, so if you are not great at

sales, it is recommended to get someone who is to join your team.

2. Must focus on educational or charitable profit and cannot profit those who created the organization: You will be limited to what type of business you can open as a non-profit.

3. All profits remain in organization: If you are looking to get rich, this is not the business for you.

4. Must qualify for a sales tax exemption: You will need to research and understand this process.

Chapter 11: Recap

There has been a lot of information listed in this book, so please use the following recap as a refresher of everything that was covered. Now is a good time to highlight or write down one or more of the types of businesses you want to explore further and compose a list of potential business ideas that you thought of while reading. Knowledge means little without action, and I encourage you to take your first step at this time. What jumped out to you? What fits with your interests and values? What are your own business ideas?

1. Bricks and Mortar: Physical Location

    Pros: Meet needs in area, easy to drive traffic, engaged in the community

    Cons: Costs, location and time

2. Online or Homebased: Any type of business based online

    Pros: Low cost, freedom in schedule and location, can reach large audience

    Cons: Hard to drive traffic, hard to get sales, lots of competition

3. Franchise or Existing Business: Buying into an existing business or existing name

    Pros: Less work to get it started and build a brand, established customers, can be successful

    Cons: Less freedom, can experience resistance, can run into unexpected problems, expensive

4. <u>Creative:</u> Any business in which you sell something you create

   Pros: Creative freedom, fulfillment, joy, ability to develop following and high profits

   Cons: Marketing may feel uncomfortable, potential criticism, time-consuming

5. <u>Affiliate Marketing/Internet Marketing:</u> Make income by referring customers to others' products or services

   Pros: Inexpensive, don't have to worry about creating your own products or services, great way to support blogs and other creative ventures

   Cons: Lots of competition, sometimes low commissions, need knowledge of marketing and SEO

6. <u>Selling Products:</u> Selling physical products in exchange for money (online, in person or both)

   Pros: Create new products, can be fun, potentially lucrative, lots of different options

   Cons: High costs, time-consuming, inventory and manufacturing, legal considerations

7. <u>Service Based:</u> Provide service in exchange for payment

   Pros: Start small and grow, can capitalize on skills, can eventually train and manage others

   Cons: Time commitment, figure out how you will retain customers, invoices

8. Information Based: Selling information in exchange for money

    Pros: Many ways to sell, passive income, freedom in schedule, can profit on knowledge and experience while helping others

    Cons: Lots of competition, need to spend time and effort gaining trust, knowledge of teaching skills and marketing needed

9. Better Way to Do Things: Selling a product or service that helps provide a better way of doing things

    Pros: Can be passive or active, possibly lucrative, lots of options, often low overhead

    Cons: Need to find customers, can be time-consuming, might not be able to scale or expand

10. Nonprofit: Conducts business for general good, not for profit

    Pros: Qualify for grants, are able to have salaried employees, volunteers help keep money in corporation, and can change the world!

    Cons: Can be stressful and time consuming to find and obtain funding, must sell your mission, limited in what you can open, cannot profit.

Conclusion

Thank you for purchasing this book and taking the first step to start your perfect business. This introductory book was written with the intention of giving a brief overview of various types of businesses and to be used as a starting point for future entrepreneurs. If one or more of these business models are of interest to you, I encourage you to continue your research on them. You can find books, read blogs, search YouTube, check out related websites, and possibly sign up for some courses. The more knowledge you gain, the more confident you will become in your ability to start and run the business that is a perfect fit for you. I wish you all the best and good luck!

If I can ask you the favor of taking a minute to leave a review, I would greatly appreciate it! I always love to hear about my readers' situations and thoughts on the book. Thank you!

Have you read the two additional books in the *Business Startup for Newbies Series* yet?

This series contains everything you need to know about the mindset and habits you need for success, a step-by-step guide for starting a business, and how to prevent failure.

Business Startup for Newbies Book 1: Seeds of an Entrepreneur

Is This Book Right for Me?

If you want more out of life but are unsure of the next steps, you are tired of working a 9-5 job with little room for advancement, want more freedom, want more money, want to discover what you are passionate about or if you want to learn how to turn your passions into a successful business this book will help you.

What Will I Learn?

You will learn how to turn your values, skills and knowledge into a successful business, even if you do not have any business ideas yet. Once you develop some ideas, you will then learn techniques to ensure your ideas will be profitable. There will be lessons and activities to overcome any doubts and fears so that you feel confident to take that next step. Furthermore, you will learn how to transform your mind and habits into those of a successful entrepreneur.

How Will This Book Actually Help Me?

This book presents much more than simple business facts and figures. Every chapter first gives you information and ideas to help you understand basic concepts. This is followed by examples and case studies of fellow entrepreneurs to help further your understanding of these concepts. Finally, each chapter ends with 'Action Steps' that you will take to implement what you learned. You are able to personalize all of the information to your own situation and each chapter will get you closer to developing the habits and mindset that you need for success.

After Reading This You Will:

1. Have a clear idea of your perfect business and how to make it successful
2. Change your mindset and overcome barriers
3. Develop habits that set your life up for success

Business Startup for Newbies Book 2: Startup Essentials

About the Book

It can be stressful to think about starting a business. There is so much that goes into it and finding a place to start can be very overwhelming. This simple guide goes through all the components you will need to know to start any business (online, retail, small business, home-based). It was written by someone who was in your exact same position, only a couple of years ago. It breaks down difficult concepts into simple, actionable steps that you can apply today. It also provides credible links to free resources for additional information, webinars, and templates needed to start a business (not affiliated with author or book).

Who Will Benefit from this Book?

Anyone who: has dreams of owning a business but feels overwhelmed at the thought of starting one, who has an idea and wants to know the steps to turn it into a profitable business, who wants an exact breakdown of the steps needed to start a business. This book is intended for those without extensive business knowledge. It is meant for the lay person who wants to start a business but does not know how.

What You Will Learn

You will learn: 1.) How to develop a profitable idea 2.) Reality of starting a business today 3.) Steps and resources to research business ideas and competition 4.) Business structures and which structure is right for you 5.) How to work with lawyers, accountants, employees and other professionals 6.) Simple tax breakdown 7.) Steps to financial planning 8.) Options to fund your business 9.) The right way to market and brand your business 10.) A simple guide to create a business plan.

How This Book is Different

- 1.) Uses simple, concrete language and examples to break down hard concepts.
- 2.) Gives an overview of all types of businesses and helps you figure out the right fit.
- 3.) Gives reader actionable steps to succeed instead of simply reciting facts

About the Author

I sat on the trolley every morning and evening commuting to and from work. To a job that required a Master's degree. A job that took six years in school with a 4.0 GPA and six months after graduating with my M.A. to get. A job that I moved and bought a house for and was very excited to begin. A job that quickly sucked the life out of me, yet I continued to work at for over four years. So, for over four years, I sat on that trolley and looked at the fellow commuters. They all looked miserable. I would sit there every day thinking *I do not want to be riding on this trolley for the remainder of my working years.* Nevertheless, I sat there year after year and never made a change. Often my co-worker and I would talk about the businesses we would want to open and how fun it would be to live a life other than one where we dreaded work each day. It always seemed like a nice dream to fantasize about but one that never seemed in reach. I remember telling my supervisor in grad school I just wanted a job I looked forward to working each day and she scoffed at the seemingly naïve comment. It seemed I always had this feeling there was more out there but I did not know what it was.

It was not until I moved to a new city that a shift began. I moved for a new, happy life but soon fell back into old routines, applying for jobs I was not passionate about for salaries far beneath what I wanted. A simple discussion with my boyfriend, in which he stated there should be more pet stores in our dog-friendly area, prompted my mind shift. I love animals. I had money from selling my house and I could be the one to open this pet store!

I began to explore opening a bricks and mortar pet boutique. The neighborhood I lived in was full of dogs and I was confident it would be a success. I went to the library and started to search for books about business. They all seemed so boring and dry, until I found one that drew me in. Through reading this book, I learned that people from all walks of life, with different passions, have been successful opening their own businesses. This gave me a boost of confidence.

I found a local non-profit that offered business classes for those interested in starting their own businesses (www.score.org). I went through a 6 week course and was excited about continuing on this journey. To get experience in management, I became a manager at a coffee shop and also a dog walker while I continued to plan and look for store locations. I found out quickly, that I did not like managing. I was always on call. I remember taking a weekend trip and getting 5 calls on the way up from employees. This made me begin to question what it would be like if I opened up my own place. It made me a little uneasy to think about not having the freedom to enjoy a weekend away when I wanted. While this was happening, I was also not having any luck finding a location for a store in my area. In talking with my business mentor, I decided it would be a good idea to look into starting an online store while I continued to look for locations. I began to research this a bit further and realized it would be feasible. I had to, however, make an entirely new business plan. I began this process planning for a physical location but online was a new beast.

My online pet boutique was up and running within a few months of me making this decision. It is not initially easy to drive traffic to an online business but I began to see the potential of having a business based online. There was freedom in this. I could work from anywhere and make my own schedule. Every single day, I read tons of information, watched YouTube videos instead of TV, and listened to business podcasts in the car, instead of the radio. I also began a personal journey that involved intense work on my anxieties and mindset. I learned about manifesting and subconscious reprogramming, and applied the techniques. I became very honest with myself about what I truly wanted, and what personal traits and thoughts were holding me back from this. In the course of a year, I completely transformed.

I loved to tell my friends and family all the things I was learning and applying. I had some hiccups with my online pet boutique, due to manufacturer issues, and during this time re-evaluated what I truly wanted to do. Selling adorable animal products is fun but I wanted something more. Many online entrepreneurs have several businesses and I began to ponder what I could do next. I kept hearing about people fulfilling their "life purpose" and contemplated what that would look like for me. With my background in Psychology and Counseling, I felt compelled to help others. What a waste it would be for me to spend hours every day learning and developing all of these business and self-improvement techniques and not share them with anyone. Then I received a sign.

I was doing dishes, binge watching YouTube videos, when a video came on about writing and publishing books. I have always loved to write. As I sat down and watched the video and I was filled with excitement. I then searched for more free information online. I found Facebook groups where I learned from others doing this. I purchased several courses before beginning on this adventure. Everything about it just felt *right*. I can help others, use my formal background and education in Psychology, all my experience in starting and running a business, and do something I felt passionate about.

I understand that becoming an entrepreneur is about overcoming internal barriers as much as it is overcoming external barriers. My goal is to teach others how to overcome both. I share this long journey of mine to let you know it is not always a simple and straight road to success, but with the right tools and mindset you can get there. I hope to provide much more information with you on your road to success. Please reach out by signing up to my email list and shooting me a message about your current situation, triumphs, and struggles.

www.ingramcontent.com/pod-product-compliance
Lightning Source LLC
Chambersburg PA
CBHW070402190526
45169CB00003B/1081